On Earth As It Is

Michael Todd Steffen

Červená Barva Press
Somerville, Massachusetts

Červená Barva Press
P.O. Box 440357
W. Somerville, MA 02144-3222

www.cervenabarvapress.com

Bookstore: www.thelostbookshelf.com

Cover art: Bridget Galway

Cover design: William J. Kelle

ISBN: 978-1-950063-17-8

Library of Congress Control Number: 2021950743

ACKNOWLEDGMENTS

My warm thanks to the editors of the following journals where the listed poems, some in part or in earlier versions, first appeared.

POEM, "Poem for Rachel Carson" and "1967"

The Lyrical Somerville, "Generation Whatever"

Boston Area Small Press and Poetry Scene, "The Dentist"

The Poetry Porch, "Lady with the Book" and "Red, White and Blue"

The Red Letter Poem Project, "Walleye"

Muddy River Poetry Review, "Western"

Ibbetson Street, "Goodwill" and "For the Sequoias"

Bagel & Bards Anthology 2021, "For a Cranberry"

Synchronized Chaos, "You Only Live Once" and "Goodnight"

The Boston Globe, "You Owned Yourself"

Constellations, "Creature in the Livingroom"

#PeetMeNotLeave Facebook Marathon, "Climb to Climber," "The Tortoise and the Hour," and "Ansel Adams"

TABLE OF CONTENTS

On Earth As It Is

Sit With This Uneasiness

Little vessel of my soul,
sit with this uneasiness
tied to the wharf.

A big gull wheels to land
and lose its ease.

Your tackle and sails are stowed
under the threaded and knotted eyes of the canvas.

The wind wakes. The water begins to chop.
Ropes groan. Stern and bow knock, knock.

The Super-id

The sea

ever wagged by its tail.
It's all continuum, seals playing
out into their horror of an orca's play
with little mind for manners, appearance,
"plasticity," the business
of the sails of cloud
stacked like the coasts' glass mountains,
these Aeolian beings, drawing from it
fertile rain, shimmering nets
and devastating storms. Great
unselfconsciousness swims
between one's hunger and another's
from deep memory
clear to the shallows of our shellfish.
And our muck, threatening its copious
data of marvels. And unmasking me,
boy wizard on the shore
of the ponderous metaphor.

Poem for Rachel Carson

...Jot question marks
           next to Adam

and the garden grown eerily
           other. Doodle a frown
                      face by the passage

all about Prometheus and his
           beneficial
                      then rampant fire.

Even Linda Lear's magnificent
           biography
                      leaves the thief in me

wanting data from the isles
           of your sirens.
                      You could no more

confuse yourself
           with the subject of your
                      life writing than a starling

with a starfish. What species
           largely mimetic
                      would not

overwhelm
           the instances
                      of its genius

among easily taken
           human society stemmed
                      in the planet's

nature, in its inalienable
           difference,
                      vulnerable to our want

and oversight,
        we the seers
                no less having to lie

in the bed we make
        in this semiconscious
                abundance amid seas,

spring—life needing of all things
        a writer's style to bring it
                to life in our wonder.

Lady with the Book

Listen. It's a painting. Her unworldly
eyes, they look as though they've been in
the fine print of this book since it was written.
The painter's seen our infant Lord is hardly
the word in the beginning, rather unlordly
in his dismay. Although it's not uncommon
even today for mothers and their children
to fall in with a book. The theme's already
lasting in the sense that it transcends
the time of Botticelli. Surely he
sat reading with his mother in her lap
whose warmth nestled his body. In the mind's
the reach between us, though. Her fingers keep
turning the pages. *Look. Look there*, she says. *See?*

Climb to Climber

For the Mulberry whose silkworms
wove a road from China
to the Mediterranean
kimono by kimono.

By way of mere winds, by way
of the intestines of animals,
trees have traveled, John Muir
observed, with us the earth around.

Even by way of the carpentry
of ship-builders, who improvised
their trade for Christ, framing
naves for churches. Look up
in an old cathedral and notice
the upside down hull of a ship
urgent with angels,

the clouds they emerge from
good as any basis.
                          When you
stumble where the sidewalk heels up
with the wandering roots of a tree
jolting the frame in you, is it
without intention—nobody
there—heating your cheek
for the shade cast over you,
the high leaves jeering in a breeze?

You Only Live Once

"but if you do it right, once is enough,"
said Mae West to the tall man, looking up,

her hand poised on the ample curve of her dress's
hip, which in the day was thought to be sexy.

"You know," she said to him, "I lost my reputation
and I never found it."

With a little wiggle, she continued, "Hey
you handsome devil you, just how tall are you?"

The moment grew very gentle between them,
each grinning, his cheek a little red

suggesting a rural upbringing. "Why, mam,"
he said, "all of six foot six inches."

"Goodness," she breathed, wiggling again.
"You know," he said, "it's not easy for a man

over six foot, needing to bend at nearly
every door frame." Simmering

the saucy dame raised a brow. She said to him,
"It's not the feet that interest me. It's those inches."

Snake

Tail, neck. It's a member of itself,
extension to eyes. It's a mouth

alive by its severed tongue that tastes the air,
sighted by glimpses, vanishing, of what all

lies beyond my ordinary senses,
outside the savoir of the myths of old

even to Gilgamesh from whom
a sea serpent stole the sprig of eternal life

to shed its dying skin and be resown.

My each interface, unawares,
with a snake, crawls. Frightens, is fascinated.

By turns a handler and loather myself. A climber,

a creeper. A coiler, a dangler. Icy starer.

~   ~   ~

Self-ordained
George Went
Hensley with his three names
in 1909 rejected Modernist liberalism
and Freud, exclaiming,
"Read it for yourselves! The Good
Book, Mark 16, verses
17 and 18: *In my name
they shall take up serpents.*" An oak cask
stood as a sort of altar. Removing the lid
he reached into the barrel and drew
from its dark mouth a live writhing
timber rattlesnake, awing them.

"The rush in your hearts, brethren,

calls you to your faith. In accordance with
the good word, now come up
and exercise that faith
by taking up these serpents"—some dozen
of them in the cask, woven
and seething.
                                Eventually,
the observant communities
asked Hensley to pack
his things, and his snakes.
He went to Kentucky, then Florida,
leaving a trail of his literalist
followers dead of venom.

Womb Tomb

Opened to close.
Born to die.
Ashes to ashes,
blossom to seed.
I sow my grain in stone
on a short winter day
far north where the sun
rises to set.

Hello. Later.

I search to go blind.
For more, hanging onto less.
Variorum to monotony.
Multiplicity's strategy, the empty hand.

My perplexity simplifies.
I plainspeak the paradoxes.
Riddle the commonplace.
A suicidal vegetarian.

Tribute to retribution.
Scorpion stinging the tortoise
half way across.

Still born, and born again
till the point stills.

Space plummeting round and around me.

And land, at five p.m.

The Vice of Innocence

lies in its half-hearted betrayal
of the group's only prayer
for mercy,

prides itself in its certainty
of denial
to allow the seasons to
turn,

following its leaf-strewn path
on the way to its narrow salvation
deeper in the woods.

Death

We live our lives with
this certainty which in most cases
we cannot keep in front of us.
It is the ocean taking our bucket

of water, the itch beyond our reach,
knowing better than to scratch much
despite the vanity of its obsession
shared by philosophy and prime time.

It vows furtively to open the lock
that holds each of us in our cells—
with icy, fleeting intimations.
Unlike its final long gaze into our eyes.

Please Recycle

Reading an object
yields its info

to ground the mind from another
insoluble debate
with the real thing

flexibly surrendering
to your fingers' squeeze,
its tongue of fizz
deepthroating you.

Eyes watering. And to think,
zero calories, unthinkable for
the beaches of the Pacific
which have ground teeth of glass
to bevel smooth
worry amulets for the thumb,

on the label
with winding arrows of earth's clock

this worded out
reflection
of nature's modest request
to be original.

All Imagery

It seems all imagery without a story
watching these flakes of snow fall in the window
while people talk about global warming.

Who would know but that tomorrow morning
comes with surprise weather to renew the news?
The images keep changing. What's the story?

End of the world, now shouldn't that be alarming?
Keep busy, business says. Nobody knows.
It's just a lot of hoopla, this global warming.

My neighbor's selling his winter house in Florida.
"Summer can hibernate with us in Scarborough.
I'll move mother and her TV up a story

and ad the ground floor out for rent as *Roomy,
inexpensive, with a beachfront view,*
haha, to some dumbass in denial about global warming."

The dire poem, how dare it be charming?
The reader ought to feel as much as know.
Or it's just imagery without a story
like the earth turning after global warming.

The Tortoise and the Hour

Years ago an American Indian friend told me that life is actually seven times slower than the way we live it. Go figure.
—Jim Harrison

Seeing one now and then trudging along
one of the inlet roads, you grin to think
of Aesop—and the hare's path we are on
busily, with our own fables to thank

about progress. In a geological hour,
we have been warned, lacking any common
purpose, we're racing back to the ocean's floor.
Out of perspective, nature *writes* such dramas

never mind the frenzy on the beach
under the moonlight where scavenger gulls
flock to the baby crawlers as they hatch
clambering seaward. Who of us but feels

the race between the animal and time—
sown in the ruptured sand starting the chase.
Urged by the insistent clock the world becomes,
our hands reach to *the expanding universe*,

the buried egg outgrown to be scaled through
to first survival…onto limber life.
As for the hours, there are never enough
for the hound's yearning instincts: *chasing two,*

catching neither, after the old Greek
proverb. That's our heritage. No human
can hope for the zero hour a tortoise keeps
cradled in the pickle of the ocean.

17

Live

What better to tell them who tend only
to watch the dance floor from a table
by the wall? Not that poets with
their metaphor, *to seize*—

or is that irony?—typify the favorite
in the lopsided match between the heart's
leap and its endurance.

Ansel Adams

Hawk of vision, his hunger was
to appraise his subject on earth as it is,
not narrowing for extraction.
His focus widened for inclusion, vista
with the subtle artifice
of 11 "zones" of gray and pallor
enhancing features
in what we laymen simply deem
classic black and white.

So much of what he aspired to *take*
and therefore leave was land on land
on land, an edition of views of a nearly
alien planet, earth as other. Insleeve?
Back cover? Where even was the photographer's
picture? Bowl of valley? Aerialist pines?

His millennially worn pristine meccas
and reclining foothills
powerfully magnetized compositions.
His dalliance with sagebrush blurred
in ankle breezes.
His patience and rigor couldn't keep
the clouds from being capricious—
wisp to flock to castle.

Let the poet call his subject the iconic West
in her bones of weather.
What could be sweeter
than all of these intimacies of her sleep?
What more thrilling and desired
than her incipient tantrums
in an indecision of clouds
over a glacial mountain?

Geology

All the moment has is arguments,
the truth unravels to contradict us—

subject of purest reflection,
unhinged from prediction, predication,

predation
which geology records

in rock,
history of aftermath

telling us like *Genesis*
the garden was well stacked before our first parents

and that what has been
has been again and again

while time's unique utterances
keep vanishing

from their mutant forms
under layers of dust,

some of it
in droplets of amber.

I yawp.

Word of word's opposite,
of earth, loom of stuff—

ice shelf to
inland sea excavation,

book written over
overwritten footprints

of civilizations, braided
tail swallowed again

by the mouth of matter
crystalizing our trash,

grain of sand
chaffing to pearl, brushstroke

suddenly divulging
the substantiated rest of the story,

immensity I sleep on.

Orientation

Widely spaced the chairs facing the wall
opposite the sunset window.

A hat box over the one lamp's head.
The sofa tilted vertically in the corner.

You called it "live-in message art"
with the title *Parlor 2006*.

Generation Whatever

In the old album of the photographs
that you took more than twenty years ago
a cloth of peppermint burns with night's stars,
a dog retrieves a disc, Beethoven's *Ode
To Joy*. Out of focus—upside down?—
the subjects, if barely recognizable,
endure the image taker's (maker's?) fierce
resistance to fulfill any expectation.
Plates and glasses under an empty table
are placed in candlelight. Why that was done
I should know better than to ask, yet am
at a loss now to remember the occasion—
bronzed as it were in havoc meant for laughs.
But then ask anything to stand with time.

The Body Fluid

From the body stone dreamt by Rodin
The Thinker, solemn as this one emerged

with his thighs slightly spread for balance
to lean this elbow on this knee

and prop chin on knuckles (the ruminant's
teeth clenched firmly now to elevate

his ruminations). The story the static
image has to tell must be imagined

before and after. Before one sat thus
one must have crawled, a life as piecemeal

as chisel on stone, day after day after day
to come to this pose in the museum

where some snarky tourist walks by
and confides to the masterpiece, *Shit, my man,*
or get off the pot. Haha.
                                    But this is only
half the story, my man.
                                    Vision will not
turn and turn and turn only on what

has been. There must be a life to come.
Where the figure's rising and some third

dimension (winds of distance) brings rain,
a hissing shower that would prompt the created

machine of consideration to somewhat
own a self, and do anything to stand up.

Skin

Organ whose music surrounds me
holding me in, keeping me together,
I note how we, like any other,
wrinkle at hand, brow and knee

where work and emotion have worn,
walking and sitting have bent.
My name and thoughts have paid you rent
without fail since I was born

taught by stove and thorn's prick
you're thin enough to make me cry.
Yet to get under us, the eye
of day and rumor runs us thick.

Fingernails

Lady, you filed
and polished, drew the animal's
weapons. You stood my flesh
to its groomings. Yes.

But when I shook
hands with the folk singer,
the long hard fingernails
kept to pick guitar strings

rang the forgotten music
of survival into my palm,
the threat
in the accompaniment

outstripping admiration
with something in my gut
that called me squeamish
hypocrite of audience

entranced by the cry
but blind to the life
and death struggle
of creation. Still

in denial with incisors
I gnaw at the ancestral
stubs, with tongue
smoothing a blunt edge.

The Barber

He was meant to touch you. With his humor he knew
to make a comfortable distance of his nearness,
setting his hand light on your shoulder, meeting
your look back through the wall-wide mirror.

Moving with stealth and reserve like a thief
he was quietly aware (although
he was professional, got paid for it)
he was taking something of yourself from you,

keepsake as the grief which made a small boy
wince in the outsized leather chair, the clipped
locks of your person shedding
into the lashes of pink watery eyes.

Easy with this intimacy
he chewed mint gum and smelled of aftershave
joking with the assistant at the next chair—
glance for glance in the mirror, with winks of complicity

nudging your shoulder, the metal of
his scissors steadied cold up behind the ear
angled, snipping—wiping your neck deftly
with a scented soft brush. Seconds ticked

with the poised contact of his waist up against
your elbow, for modesty suffering him
to operate in your sensible sphere, and to grin
with that far-off squint, just run of the day.

The Dentist

with his little extended
circle of a mirror
reached into your darkness,

with his fine sharp metal hook
mining for resistance—and decay.
As if the x-ray hadn't shown him.

Who puts their fingers
in your mouth?—a layer of us
wonders, reclined in his uneasy chair,

with his concentration
of a chess player to situate
or remove, drill, crown…

Under the angelic vanity:
my jaw spiked with reminders
of the original skull, our dust

whose agony won't outlast
though bites down to measure
now—ow!—invention of

the moment and its isolating
pain in the more plausible
"rib" of Adam God removed

like a lisp
of self-cultivated shrapnel,
that we be recognizable

among peers
with enough missing from our smile.

Over the Rainbow

Having broken that light barrier
where elemental colors band
as in the promise of code, equation,
you would need reading glasses.

Distance with perspective transcended,
nothing in your reach could come into focus.

No, this wouldn't look like Kansas
anymore.
               On its throne
of absence, the self would occupy you
with the opposite curse of Midas'—
everything you picked up turned into
a mirror with its reflection of you
searching, surrounded by *Lumières*
with everything knowable made
encyclopedic,

a great song and dance in the fracture
enabling the takeover of farce.

Nothing else could be itself. The plain
brick road could only be yellow.

Dog Gone

Where are you tonight,
my patchy Dalmatian with
your wet nose's nudge?

For Galway Kinnell

1927 - 2014

You followed a set of footprints aimed for the woods
days in the news of you, in the ongoing
life of your words, though for another poet
going as if to die among "those dark trees"—
in January's biting snow to make me
shiver—confused by actual weather,
skies blue, barely needing a sweater
in late October. Your sleeper's scare
was the world's bad sleep, tracing our otherly
mortal truth.

If there were time. We go forever
too soon and late at once, you tracking off
hindered in a snowfall that hadn't snowed yet,
complaining with us still: *Why do you talk so much,*
Robert Frost? One day I drove up to Ripton to ask...

Being woken, being troubled animals
wrested speech from the tongue.
We predicate nothing
that isn't ongoing, only confirm
as tacit order the cruel
which sanity as random happening cannot accept.
We need an angel to tell us this is so.

Let the entertained
bill the piper. Long after life
stole them back from your art, we burn our fingers
on the sticks of tramps' fires, ever curious
about what had led them. The dizzy spiral of
the universe's harmonies had formed
the conch of our ears already.

For an Osage Orange Tree

whose fruit is green
caught out as Mock; fiber
deemed chief for weapons and called Bowwood;

discovered by the botanist Nuttall who Latinized
it after a friend as *Maclura pomifera*—
like a flag on a moon. Also Prairie Hedgeplant,
Yellowwood.
                    It leaves me
silent and astonished as a tree
that no true name pierces the language bubble

but that things and lives just are, assumed
and attributed to *there* or *them*, beggars
of utterance in their differences, forever mistaken.

1967

The news was Vietnam, riots in Buffalo
And Jayne Mansfield. Walter Cronkite
Telling us about it wouldn't change a thing.
Yet the TV stayed lit at uncle Jack and aunt Donna's

Through the summer evenings I stayed with them
A-h-h-h-ing into the whirling metal blades
Of the electric fan where my voice broke up
Into ribbons of staccato. "Mind your fingers,"

Aunt Donna warned and sipped from her iced tea,
The glass beaded with sweat. It is so present,
The smell of wet dog imbuing the shag carpet,
The dust on the shelves with the family photos

In guilt-glass frames, one of an enshrined uncle
Lost in World War II. The slap of cards
In rummy suits coming from the kitchen table
With Cronkite's muted mustache lip-syncing—

Since aunt Donna preferred KYMN,
Portland's "Fine Kim" hit music station
—Conway Twitty's undeniably swallowed
Refrain of denial, *It's only make believe…*

Red, White and Blue

Barns, snow, evening sky
filling with stars. Strawberries, piano fores,
the glittering scales of little plump fish

twitching on our lines in the shallow lake.
Stop sign, blind of eye, new Levis.
Clay, fuzzy dandelions (in things

even this tenuous with their least
grip in the bend of ideas), grass of Kentucky.
Wing of blackbird, cascade, full full moon.

Walleye

In the gray areas, at dawn or dusk,
or in the "chop" of lakes on windy days
walleye feed only where they're advantaged
by the vision of their eye which in fact

protrudes as though beaming at a wall.
My friend's father, a banker, would leave
his banker's hours some weekends
to come home late Sunday afternoon

scruffy, haggard and smelly, a banker's
opposite, with coolers full of crushed ice
and gutted walleye with the heads—
like pike toothed agape in token menace,

like perch with fanned double back fins.
Only like themselves agog in either
genuine remorse or resentment, god knew.
Our homes that took in the sportsman's

generosity were at first aromatized hazily
by herbs and the crumbly flesh sautéed in butter—
that finally left a stubborn stink.
Slept, shaven, in his suit and tie again

he'd drive back off for his desk at the bank
with his windshield glinting under the sun
and blue sky that drove the walleye
away from the shoreline back to the deep end.

Leaving College

I had to pay off the electric bill
for the studio apartment
I was privileged to live in my senior year
and was in a dither about
how to fit my tennis racquets
into the back seat of my VW
jammed with boxes of books
as if closed for good, not my only
held illusion heading into "the real
world." I was grinning at a card
from a rancher uncle in Western
Nebraska, congratulating me
for being no damn better
than one of them January days
that turns your lips blue
now that I had one degree.

Western

The suns of my shadow set on old westerns
the way I still get into it,
tensing at the gunfights, clutching, wincing
as the actors to their wounds. The whisper of
look out to the sheriff who's being snuck up on
in the abandoned one street of the town—
the shadow flitting from the General Store
to crouch behind an unhitched wagon.
There is the strike of a match
on the boot heel to light the outlaw's cigar,
bringing tension to our breathing
in the wild country of sage brush and rock formations.

In this one they wear two-day
beards with greasy sweat on their faces
holding their pistols, looking out the windows
while ma and pa sit with their arms and legs
tied by ropes to chairs in a sparse décor—
table, wood stove, shelf with books and trinkets
—evoking home on the range.

The strangely good guy is on his way.
From out there in the dark of night his bullet
will report through one of those windows. The bandits
will break the rest of the glass out with their pistols
to shoot back at him. Here in the living room
though the movie's growing close, with those two
bound to surrender, the other two to be freed,
we grip the recliners' cushions, digging in
for the resistance of the shoot-out,
not quite ready to go to bed.

For a Cranberry

Summertime for us
holding out beneath
the stars, your tender voice
and storm inside your breath

perched on a compact disc
flying off of it, enchantress
of range, alto to brusque,
coquettish, dear, defiant.

Angels see everything,
the love, the grief, the gall
that transform life to song.
Cross woman and Tom girl

of bogs and their bright fruit
waded in to gather,
on the tongue bitter and sweet.
Dolores O'Riordan sang here.

Going to Bed

Best not even raise the question how long
the book you've just closed will take to darken
on the bed stand under the lamp you've just
put out. You don't even wonder whether
you've closed your eyes. You keep seeing things
in the spectrum of the language in your mind
now and then surfacing to the present
like a swimmer for air, to pull off your tee-shirt
because even with the fan blowing
you feel too warm. And to find
the low rumble of the plane taking off odd
this late at night, perhaps with next-day
cargo. Driving down a country road
in Oklahoma once you pulled over to take
a leak and far away from the city's lights
looked up to marvel at the stars in thick
clusters, as probably we would look
to heaven if we had fire in our DNA
like lightning bugs, an idea that changes
positions to find comfort with the body
lying here in its almost nightly rehearsal
of death, which would similarly wonder
where we are headed, were it not that we are
already mercifully caught up in going there.

Goodwill

We give ourselves away. We give the shirts
styled for a decade, donned a day, still wearing
tags—*Dockers, Dior*—of selves
outgrown or only glanced at, to hang
for bargainers' scrutiny on tight racks. Will
choosers be beggars for looks
in the mirror, thumbs up
in hand-me-downs? We browse for pocket
rather than collar or cuff, digging
our treasures from others' discards,
itch as they may. Finders
keepers, with wide eyes: *Can you believe...*
as simultaneously across town
with equal remorse: *How could I have
let go of that Polo?* Of the senses
(with cents) you count, your taste
for plums comforts others. Your touch
withdraws in the XLs. Your eyes
are burning holes through me. More dire
acceptance steps softly. *If the shoe fits—*
Cinderella, Seuss, disguised for the meanwhile.

You Owned Yourself
—for Mel Jenkins 1956 - 2014

Every time I saw you it was raining.
On your milk carton in front of the Harvard Book Store
Holding your paper cup out, stemming for rain,
Your joke was ever timely and the same
And with sacred reference: *My cup overfloweth.*

You'd come in from the street
Bringing the rain, your constant friend
Of bitterness that had prepared you for
The friendliness of every other thing
And made your humor all-weather, all of the time.

Like the sidewalk you sat on, the only way
For you to look was up. You had learned this.
Several others around you just quit trying
To see beyond themselves. They cast their inward
Silence. Whereas you, Mel, would never

Shut up, even when we'd ask you to,
Me and the other guys watching Law & Order.
Especially when we'd ask you to be quiet
You'd raise your voice, grinning, as though to be heard
Through the rain over you crashing into a downpour.

To a Housefly in Winter

Odd and obvious
for the season,
you could've hibernated
till milder spring.

But life's abundant
unfairness hatched you
to ess through our heated
corridors the month

of your span, in innocence
eluding
William Blake's
thoughtful brush of hand.

I've read that
your compound eyes process
sights seven times
quicker than I,

seeing *in slow motion*
with your *higher*
flicker fusion rate...
That you taste

with your legs
before your probiscus
like a trunk in the pond
of a drop of cola

constitutes your liquid diet.
Near your claws there are
adhesive pads, *pulvilli*,
facilitating your walk

on walls and ceilings
with glorious
agility
having its own sorrowful

demise, betokened by one
of your forebears,
a partial wing left,
flat on his back

in the window sill.
Beyond the thin transparency
full of light attracting you,
you must feel the confine

I clothe myself
to step out of, into
my own wondrous machine's
transitory clinging.

Creature in the Living Room

Omen.
Fluttering under the curtain rail—
revealing tail feathers, a clutching talon . . .

With blind concentration
chasing—following around
a totally other will
to get away.
Come here... No, over here...

You mistake the light
in the picture window's glass
for free open sky—
knocking yourself dazed,
ever more panicked.

Desperate me—afternoon
falling, soon to be dark—
what among the vases,
photo frames or occasional
dining set must be broken?
—trying to coax you into a laundry net,

wary of your beak. Your wing.

Buggy

the feet of an ant make their own sound on the earth
—Jane Hirshfield, "Mosquito"

Before I read about them, cricket
and ant, genus and species,
walk all I wanted
they were always in my path
in the long grass hopping, landing, swarming
at the intersections
of my world and theirs.

The summer day long by the lake
I'd hear them humming, droning, chirring.
I'd lower my pointing finger
toward the backward forceps of an earwig
daring its pinch?—
scratching the cave of my ear with my finger.
All through the night: the crickets' stridulation
listened and listened to, long before heard.

Ancient Greek coins from Ephesus
held representations of bees
those domesticated workers
whose honey sweetened my breakfast toast
and breakfast tea.

Before I read Nabokov,
novelist and lepidopterist,
his butterflies made
earthly psychology
while the wonder of Kafka's Gregor—
was it all in the head
of anyone who couldn't get out of bed?

From the old cave depictions people
used smoke already to mollify bees
enabling taking their honey
with less risk of being stung.

A small white lump formed on
the tanned backside of my hand
near the king's knuckle
where the mosquito's violin tuned
into a needle and drew in.
It itched and itched
and I scratched the thinned layer
until it bled and left a more obvious scab.

Of disproportionate lives:
the blue moon, an Australian cicada,
lives underground, feeding on roots
as a nymph for seven years
to emerge in sunlight just a few days
hissing in the shade of leaves.

I'd come upon the fly boneyard of a windowsill
to discover death's utter desertion
of the bodies, the only dutiful sweep
of them onto a newspaper to be disposed of.

Beetle, horsefly, praying mantis: must
insects be sectarian?

Deep in inner space, under the great forest
of the leaves of grass, onto which I had posed
my hand, leaning back on a summer's day
like a young character out of Ivan Turgenev,
red ants swarmed feverishly around the mound
flattened by my unknowing hand—
alerted to the stings of their defense
to want to look back through the grass to see them.

To worlds of others we are as giants,
like Gulliver fallibly outnumbered.
Gardeners and husbands that we are
we house the bee for its honey and wax,
make a great Road from China to the Mediterranean
on countless silkworms—5,000
a kimono—that feed on mulberry trees.

Hopping around shower and sink drains—
millions and millions of springtails
on a moist acre, feeding
on mold, on decay of leaves and grass,
keeping the planet uncluttered and healthy.
There's something rotten not just in Denmark.
There's rot consumption at the intersections
of worlds. Flies and their larvae,
maggots I imagined
were busy at the carcass of the coyote
lying beside the railroad in the gulch
my bus into work rode by the other day.

Thank them
the entomologists do
who enjoy etymology—
antlion, Belzebub bee-eater, camel spider,
doodlebug.

Thank you
I do, for listening in.

New Hampshire

Influences

My stars, my stars. These
invitations for me I
could only wish on.

Again

The same red oak leaves
huddled over the same stone
masonry of the old Powder House.

Soul

For only a glimpse
the moose in the small clearing.
I kept seeing him all day.

Take me out, he thought

... to the Ball Park.

                        The one day
of a summer's week
the poet at Wrigley took for himself
grew clean as the snap of leather—
stitched ball into mitt.

"If it wasn't for our pitching, fielding,
hitting and base running, we'd be
looking good,"
                        the poet lamented
to a crack of pine and the crowd's *ahhh*
watching the hit arc far foul

under the bright sun, the green field
and its trajectories oddly determined

and surreal, the lightning
of no two pitches striking the same
keeping ump and scorekeeper vigilant
with the infielders on the balls
of their feet,
                        a good three-quarters
of every minute slouched
with glove on knee, bat on shoulder
kicking around for the next pitch.

Nearly Faded

Brass to look at, the inseams
dug into the creases of sitting,
seat patch sagging to the hams
of standing around. It's hard
to tell yourself from your close fit—
belt through loops holding the stitched
leather to its tarnished buckle. The day
nous venons tous de Nîmes, hugging
as equality should, shaped to
our thighs like poultry, having heeled
the hems of our cuffs to tatters,
only a little bluer than winter's sky.
Sing along, fingers buried
to their knuckles in tight pockets.

Poetry

Tree of singing,
tree of silence.
The starlings have come and gone.

For the Sequoias

whose ancestors John Muir sought
far and wide, finding none,
bottom- and topmost turtle.

Wondering
or failing to wonder at them
because we cannot measure up,
it's easy to speak against these
high embodiments of years,
takers of our youth and loves.

They number *us*, each
deepening through brief splendors of autumn
to the long attenuation of our depth
and cover, to a nudity
who will fumble with?

Sky-bound, street-wide stepped—
30 couples waltzed on the diameter
floor of the first one felled by a gold-rusher.

As much they tell us
we shade ourselves beyond the sunken
tooth in the fruit, the promise is borne
of our ongoing need
to witness these things, being
remembered—time's tail in time's mouth—
otherwise as soon erased and lost,

the rain and the shaken leaves, the swifts in front
of the storm, the hawk in the silence after.

Bark

Calloused peel of trees,
to love some harshness.

Whatever the cat
was crying about

I scraped hands,
elbows and knees

on the rough knobby grooved outsides
struggling up for a view of things.

ABOUT THE AUTHOR

Of his first book *Partner, Orchard, Day Moon* published in 2014 David Ferry wrote, *Michael Steffen is so alive in his writing, keen with observation, both of what things actually look like, what the wind feels like, how things grow and rot, and also of character, his own, his uncles', anybody's he sees.* Steffen is the recipient of a 2021 Massachusetts Cultural Council Literary Fellowship, and his poetry has appeared in journals, including *The Boston Globe, The Concord Saunterer, Ibbetson Street, The Lyric* and *Synchronized Chaos.*